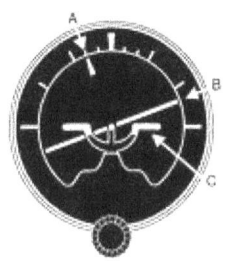

Aviation Faith Series
VOLUME 2

By Blessings Storehouse Ministries,
Author: Tarja A. Newman

Copyright © by Blessings Storehouse Ministries
Copyright © case number 1-400098192

Printed in the United States of America.
All rights reserved under International Copyright Law. Contents and/or cover may not be reproduced in whole or in part in any form without the express written consent of the publisher.

This edition published by
Blessings Storehouse Ministries.

Cover & Interior: Tarja A Newman
Comic Strips: ChickenWingsComics.com

Unless otherwise indicated, scripture quotations are taken from the *King James Version* of the Bible.

Scripture quotations marked (AMP) are taken from *the Amplified Bible*, Copyright © 1954, 1958, 1962, 1964, 1965, 1987 by The Lockman Foundation. Used by permission.

ISBN: 978-0-9826482-1-6

ATTITUDES
that bring
SUCCESS

Table of Contents

Foreword ix

Acknowledgments and Thanks xi

Introduction. xv

CHAPTER ONE

    Learning to Fly 3

    Different levels of Pilot's and
    Their Certificates 5

CHAPTER TWO

    Are you a Glider, Propeller
    plane or a Jet? 15

    Pitch, Power and Trim 21

    The Ultimate Test of a Pilot 22

CHAPTER THREE

    Mountain Be Thou Removed. 29

    Have Faith in the System 33

    What is this Density Altitude? 37

CHAPTER FOUR

    Weight and Balance & Aerodynamics . . 43

    Critical Attitude. 44

    Protect that Attitude 46

    Failed Attitudes 48

    Performance. 49

CHAPTER FIVE

    Law vs. Principle 53

    Put the Right Law in Motion. 55

    Talents. 60

CHAPTER SIX

    What's Your Destination?. 67

    Step by Step Plan 71

    Keep Your Eye on the Goal. 76

CHAPTER SEVEN

    Stages of Development 81

    Situational Awareness. 84

CHAPTER EIGHT

    Respect and Honor 89

    Tune into the Holy Spirit. 91

Wrong Signals. 93
Have Confidence 94

CHAPTER NINE
Get Ready To Be Intercepted. 101
Harvest 104
Air Force One. 107

CHAPTER TEN
In Conclusion 113

My Prayer 119
About the Author 121
Prayer of Salvation 123

Foreword

We are thrilled to have been asked by Tarja to contribute to her sequel of Aviation Faith Series. Our flight school, Airborne Systems was birthed as the result of a dream for flying and the desire to help others achieve aviation goals. It took hard work and perseverance from the founder Oney V. Ramirez (who passed away in 2009) and help and dedication of talented and devoted Instructors like Tarja to impart the knowledge and skills needed to succeed.

Many of the teachings of the Bible come into play in our day to day running of the business. Believing in ourselves and our product, ethical behavior in all our dealings, emphasis on preparedness and, treating customers and staff right have differentiated us from the competition and have made us the school of choice by many.

We applaud Tarja's love for the faith and her trade that has influenced her call to write this book. A gift that will have enormous impact to the ministries she believes in and hopefully influence readers to align their faith and actions in unison for a Greater good.

Maria L. Canosa and Vincent Billisi.
Airborne Systems Flight Schools.

Acknowledgments and Thanks

It is impossible to make a mention of all the individuals that have been influential in shaping my life and inspiring me to continue to write, for there are so many of you. However, I must always mention those closest to me. You are such an integral part of my life and such great examples to follow.

First and foremost, I must acknowledge my Lord and Savior Jesus Christ. It is because of His inspiration and out of my gratitude for Him that I am writing these Series. Since it is His project, all proceeds from the book will be given to Ministry work, to help orphans and to minister where there is need. For more information you can visit http://blessingsstorehouse.blogspot.com.

My husband Nick, as always, you are my inspiration and the biggest support in everything. You make it easy for me to pursue what I feel led to do for God. I love you so much.

My parents Elina and Juhani, you gave my brother and me the positive outlook for life by encouraging us to be and do our best and to pursue our dreams. You showed us how to work as a team to make your dreams a reality.

My brother Kuja, you also took that example seriously and pursued your dream in music and now you are an inspiration to many, including myself.

My sister-in-law Rodica, I see you always put others ahead of yourself and it is in your heart to always be the giver rather than taker.

Pastor Stan Moore from Words of Life Church in North Miami, my pastor, your teaching of attitudes started this journey of writing. You and your family has been the spark that ignited the fire, which began the Aviation Faith Series and I thank you.

Of course, I cannot leave out the awesome and so well operated Airborne Systems Flight School, where I have the privilege to spend most of my days and where I also get much of my inspiration and ideas. You guys are the most professional and yet so personable individuals. I am so blessed to have the opportunity to be associated with you all!

Once again I am so excited to thank Stefan and Michael Strasser from ChickenWingsComics.com for their contribution of comic strips for this book. You have such a great sense of humor and an awesome attitude, even when I know that life has handed you some lemons. Thanks for making the serious things in life that much lighter to deal with through your aviation humor. I encourage everyone reading this book to go visit them at www.ChickenWingsComics.com. They have a lot more lessons for life and tools to help you with attitude adjustments right on their site.

Introduction

The last book I wrote in the Aviation Faith Series was definitely a faith project. I had never authored a book, but I felt I had direct instructions from the Lord to write. I really didn't know why I was writing it, but I got so inspired by the subject following several teachings by my pastor Stan Moore from the Words of Life Fellowship Church in Miami, FL that I simply had to start writing things down. As he was teaching about the subject of Attitude and things relating to Aviation, I started to see parallels in the two and how they really related to our everyday lives and Faith. Only later would I see how this book was to be one of the many tools to be used to fund the gospel as well as bring inspiration to the body of Christ.

No sooner than when I had finished writing it, the Lord impressed upon me to continue writing as more and more revelation kept coming from the Lord and I started seeing even more parables from Aviation relating to Faith and Life. Therefore this book is the end result of that, and it is continuing the Aviation Faith Series.

I owe a lot to my pastors Stan and Geri Moore and their family for all the inspiration that has not only propelled me to writing these books, but also increased my hunger to spend more and more time with the Source Himself. They are also a big reason why Aviation is such a great part of me right now and how God has used it in my life thus far. I will never forget how I have gotten to this point in my life and how God has used my pastors in shaping my life. They will continue to be my inspiration.

CHAPTER ONE

Wisdom Nugget #1

Wise Men Learn More
From Fools Than Fools
From The Wise.

—Chinese Proverb

CHAPTER ONE

Learning to Fly

When you are learning to fly you must have someone to teach you. You couldn't just get in an airplane and fly away (unless, of course, it's someone else who was a trained pilot flying for you). If you did get in an airplane to fly yourself without any kind of training, you would most likely crash not knowing how to control that airplane. I feel the same way about the Christian life. We must have examples and teachers who to emulate. Otherwise you wouldn't know how a Christian is supposed to operate. You must also know your rights and privileges. For a Christian these are the promises and directions in the Bible and for a pilot they are the rules and regulations to follow and the Manufacturer's Operating Handbook or Airplane

Flight Manual. These can keep you out of trouble and also get you out of it should you encounter some.

You must have someone to teach you about the limits and the systems of the airplane and the aerodynamics among many other things. You also must have someone teach you about the affairs of life, like a pastor does, so that you know how to operate accordingly and keep yourself out of trouble.

Like I was mentioning in the introduction, I have been extremely blessed and inspired by my pastor and his teachings. Because of his background as a coach and a teacher, he knows how to really drive home some of the things we need to learn as the children of God and think bigger like God does. There's so much I have gotten from my pastor's teachings of favor, attitude, the protection of the shed blood of Jesus, the fear of the Lord, confessing the Word, just to mention a few. He also increased my thinking when he was sharing with us the pictures of the planets in this universe and showing how great God really is, the Creator of the whole universe. By really comparing the sizes of the planets to our little earth just made me realize how great God is and how small our daily affairs are to Him. God is bigger than anything we could ever face and there is nothing too hard for Him!

So when you are learning to fly, you must have an instructor to get you to the next level. When you move on to more advanced aircraft that requires two pilots, (like in the airlines for example,) you will have a Training Captain. A Training Captain is one that has all the experience and serves as an instructor. You are *acting* as the captain of your ship, but the Training Captain is *in charge*. He *is* the Pilot in Command. Now, you are also a captain since you are *acting as* a captain. But, the Training Captain is the one who is there to "bail you out" if you needed it. He will, however, expect you to make all the decisions and make them correctly and according to the rules and safety.

This is how it is with God. You know that He has given us free will and the responsibility to "steer" our boat - or an airplane. He has given us the authority to *act as* the captain of our lives. But, He is still the one who created all things and He is in control. He is still there to train you to make the right decisions if you just listen to Him and obey.

Different levels of Pilot's and Their Certificates

Student Pilot Certificate - This is where everyone starts, as a student. You will need to be supervised wherever you go as you are simply learning the different aspects of aviation. You are taking baby steps and advancing at your own pace. You also need a special permission from your instructor to fly solo.

Recreational Pilot Certificate - This one is a fairly new license, but it limits you from flying further than 50 miles from your destination. Also, it will not allow you to fly at night. Sounds pretty much like the Baby Christian level, where you are not really supervised any longer, but somewhat limited as you do not have the full knowledge of at least the Private Pilot level.

Private Pilot Certificate - Everyone needs to get this certificate first before advancing to getting another certificate. This is a basic certificate, but allows you to fly only in visual conditions we call VFR (Visual Flight Rules) if not additionally rated with Instrument Rating. In other words, a person with a basic Private Pilot Certificate flies by sight only and is not allowed to fly "blind" by instrument reference.

Although Private Pilot will receive some basic training in flying by the reference to instruments only, but since they are not developed in fully trusting the instruments, they are not yet allowed to go into those weather conditions where you cannot see outside.

So, to an extent, the Private Pilot without an Instrument Rating is like a Christian who flies by sight and not by Faith as they are not yet developed to fully trust the instruments, which is the Word of God.

Instrument Rating - A person with a Private Pilot Certificate may add this additional rating to his or her certificate. This will allow a person to fly in the clouds by the reference to the instruments only. We call it IFR flying, meaning flying by Instrument Flight Rules.

Instrument Rating will make any pilot much better and safer as they will learn to trust the instruments in the cockpit. Those instruments will help you maintain the airplane in the upright attitude when you do not see outside. For us as Christians those instruments are the Words in the Bible. If we keep them in front of our eyes, we can keep our attitudes in upright position. Through them we walk by Faith and not by sight.

Commercial Pilot Certificate - If a pilot considers flying professionally, he or she will need this level of certificate. Commercial Pilot Certificate will allow the pilot to be hired for variety of positions as a crew member and fly as a professional pilot. You will also advance to a different level as the training for Commercial Pilot Certificate involves handling that aircraft precisely and being so coordinated as if you were one with it. You will also gain a higher level of knowledge base as a Commercial Pilot.

This is like advancing as a Christian to the next level and proficiency. Study the Word and stay with your training so you, too, will graduate from a Private Pilot to the Commercial Pilot Level. This way God can "hire" you for an assignment when you are ready and fully trained.

While most Commercial Pilots have also the previously mentioned Instrument Rating, some do not. If you were a Commercial Pilot without the Instrument Rating, you would be limited to fly passengers only within 50 mile distance and you would not be allowed to fly them at night in commercial operations. This is because you wouldn't be fully developed in trusting your instruments yet and you would not be allowed in situations that could become a hazard to you or anyone with you.

So, if you are going by sight and not by Faith, you are not allowed to take others with you very far with a limited Commercial Pilot Certificate when you are operating "for hire". But, if you develop your trust to the instruments and get your Instrument Rating, all limits will be off for you.

Airline Transport Pilot Certificate - This is the next level after you have been a Commercial Pilot for a while and build some experience. You couldn't get this certificate overnight as it takes certain amount of flight time and experience in different types of flying before you can apply for a check ride at ATP level. This is mostly an Instrument Flying Check ride, but at a higher level.

At this level you are fully proficient trusting the instruments (walking by Faith). Your vocabulary also is very developed as you have had the opportunity to practice your words. Your flying is precise and you make competent decisions. (All your decisions are based on the Word of God).

This is the level of certificate required to operate with a Pilot in Command Authority in certain types of aircraft for commercial operations such as Airlines or On Demand Charter. It is the highest level of license which grants you the highest level of Authority pertaining to that particular ship you are commanding. At this level God can trust you to do what He is asking you to do and you have fully learned to trust in Him. Whatever He asks you to do, you'll do. You also know your Spiritual Authority in Christ and you use it. At this level God can trust you to make the right decisions and you will make them all according to His Word and Operations Standards, which is the Bible.

Certificated Flight Instructor (CFI) - This is an additional license that you can have as long as you are a pilot at least on the Commercial Pilot Level. There are three different kinds of Certificated Flight Instructor Ratings and you can have one or more. The first one is a Basic CFI. He or she can teach Private Pilot and Commercial Pilot levels. Once you add Certificated Flight Instructor Instrument (CFI-I), you can also teach pilots to receive their Instrument Rating. There is one more level and that is Multi-Engine Instructor License (MEI). This allows you to teach in a multi-engine aircraft.

Whichever level of CFI license you have, you are now a teacher and have "studied yourself approved" in the subjects you are teaching. Your job is to pass along the knowledge and experience you have so far received to the next generation of pilots and train them in the way that they should go. In a way you are a mentor to someone else whom you are leading along the path of becoming skilled in aviation, just like a Pastor and a Teacher of the Word would be sharing their revelations and knowledge of the Word with those he is assigned to.

Whichever level of license or certificate you desire to achieve, courage, commitment and consistency will get you there. If God has put something in your heart to do, go for it with the gusto! There is nothing impossible for Him to do through you. Let Him do the work, only give Him the dedication, willingness and obedience to work with.

CHAPTER TWO

Wisdom Nugget #2

Associations Have
Everything To Do With
How You're Living.

-Jerry Savelle

CHAPTER TWO

Are you a Glider, Propeller plane or a Jet?

We all have been created in the likeness of God, just like all airplanes are built after the likeness of an airplane. What I mean is that all airplanes have the same components like wings, tail, wheels and all other crucial elements needed to do what they are meant to do, which is to fly, take-off and land. However, there are many *types* of airplanes, each built after the model of their own type and much like us humans are all formed after our own parents.

There are many looks to us, just like there are many looks to the airplanes. There are also many talents and individual capabilities to us humans much like there are different capabilities to different airplanes. But, there is one thing remains the same, and it is that all of us are people and in the category of humans, created in the image of Christ. The same way, all the airplanes are in their own category and no matter what they look like, they are all created in the image of an airplane.

If we compared ourselves to a type of an aircraft, what kind would you be? Let's look at the different types of aircraft in existence. There are many kinds of them that can take you to different heights, from airships that are slow moving and gliders that have no engine power to airplanes and helicopters. Here we are going to focus on just the gliders and airplane types.

The first one is the *Glider*. There are two kinds of gliders. The simpler one is made of fabric and is called a Hang Glider. This is how I started my flying experience. In a Hang Glider you are hanging from your back attached to the glider and you direct the glider with your own weight shifts. For example, if you wanted to turn left, you shift your body to the left. If you want to turn to the right, you shift to the right. Move your body forward and the nose of the Glider will move down and descend. If you wanted the nose

Chapter Two: Are you a Glider, Propeller plane or a Jet?

to rise, you've got to shift your body weight towards the aft and the nose will lift up.

As you can see this is a very simple system and a basic one. It is so basic that you do not develop a trust for an engine as you do not have one! I still remember when I initially started to take flying lessons in an airplane, my first question to the instructor during our climb out was "where are the parachutes?" I found it hard to believe that this piece of metal was going to fly without that engine working properly, but I came to find out that you are still going to land the thing in the safest spot possible if the engine left you and you do not bail out in the air (unless, of course, we are talking about a military airplane with the possibility to eject).

The second type of Glider is just like an airplane, except that most of them do not have and engine. So the problem - or the opportunity to overcome - with the Gliders are that they must rely on outside power to be lifted up, unless they have engines installed.

Engines are like the power that is produced by the Word of God coming out of your heart and from your mouth. The Word of God then is the gasoline in your tank. Your heart is the gas tank since that's where it is released from and it gets in there through the opening of your ears and your eyes. When your tank, your heart, is full, your mouth becomes like the fuel pump what draws it out and releases the power of the Word of God and puts it to work for you.

If you are a new Christian or are not yet developed in the Word, you may be a simple Glider and are relying on an outside source to supply the lift for you. But eventually you'll want to get some engines with a gas tank and keep it filled to the top all the time. This way, whenever you need the power to fly out on an assignment, you'll have gas in the tank and are prepared in season and out of season.

We have been promised in Ephesians 2:10 that we have been *recreated* in Christ Jesus, born a new and we are *His workmanship*.

> [10]For we are God's [own] handiwork (His workmanship), recreated in Christ Jesus, [born anew] that we may do those good works which God predestined (planned beforehand) for us [taking paths which He prepared ahead of time], that we should walk in them [living the good life which He prearranged and made ready for us to live].
> - Ephesians 2:10 (AMP)

It is like we have had an overhaul and He has added to us an engine or two, which is the Power of His Word that has been given to us to use in His Name.

Unlike most Gliders all **Airplanes** have at least one engine. Some have two or more. Just like Gliders, there are many different kinds of Airplanes as well. First there are different sizes, some are smaller and some are larger. The smaller the plane is, less stable it tends to be. The larger and more developed airplanes are usually heavier and that adds to their stability. So a very important fact for us is to grow in the Word of God, to feed on His Word, developing us into a more stable person in Christ. However, there are some other factors that we want to compare and learn from and this is to compare the different *types* of Airplanes.

The most basic one is a **Propeller Airplane**. There are **regular**, normally aspirated (normally powered) propeller airplanes and there are **Turbo boosted** propeller airplanes. The Turbo boosted engines provide additional power to the engines as you climb and you can climb to higher levels.

I kind of liken this to the two levels of a Christian walk. You can be a *naturally minded* Christian who walks *by sight* or you can be *Turbo boosted Christian walking by*

Faith. We can reach much higher levels by walking by Faith, rightly dividing the Word of God.

The next level of an Airplane is a **Jet**. Every Jet has a Turbine Engine and they are *designed* to fly high. Turbojet engines produce *Pounds of Thrust* instead of just regular Horse Power and this Thrust can propel you to much higher and get you there much faster.

Because Jets do not have the propeller, there is no drag due to the moving parts in front of the engine. This drag caused by the propeller hinders to some extent the propeller airplanes moving forward, but is completely missing on a Jet engine. Yes, there is a lot of moving parts *inside* that Jet engine producing tremendous amount of thrust, but it is totally invisible to the outside eye. You can hear and see the result, though, and if you were standing in front of that running jet engine, you could be sucked in. That's how powerful it is.

The same way when you reach Jet level with the Lord, there is a lot of power that is working within you and you are getting awesome results for the Lord. You have now shed a lot of that doubt that you may have had to shake off during the early years of walking with the Lord, which was causing some undesired drag in your life hindering your progress. But now, over the years you have learned to trust the Lord and in His Word and you have become a Jet flying higher than ever before with more ease, resting in His Word.

Whether you are a Glider, a Prop Plane or a Jet at this moment, there is hope for all of us. We can all develop into a fine Jet flying high and progressing fast. All we have to do is spend time with the manufacturer and designer who knows how to develop us into that desired piece of equipment for His Glory.

Pitch, Power and Trim

When we are training new pilots to fly and airplane we teach them what each component does in the cockpit. As you can imagine, a new pilot needs to know how to set the airplane attitude where he wants it. In order to do that, he needs to know some guidelines.

We have a saying "pitch, power and trim". What this means is that in order to set the airplanes attitude, you first have to pitch it to the position you want. Pitching means you either lift the nose of the airplane higher or lower it below its current position. You then set the power setting to establish a stable climb or descend, or just a particular airspeed in level flight. After you've got the attitude you wanted, you trim the airplane and establish or set this attitude in place so the airplane keeps it without you constantly having to do attitude adjustments.

This is the same way we should deal in our lives in relation to our attitudes. Our attitude and outlook really is our own decision. The Bible has a lot to say about the attitude and we should heed to the instructions seriously. For example, the Israelites had a lousy attitude when God was leading them out of Egypt and because of their attitudes and unbelief they wondered in the wilderness for forty days. Instead of receiving God's promises many died without ever seeing what belonged to them. Don't let it be you. Trust and heed to God's Word and believe His promises. It is His living Testament given to us. Claim those promises!

The Ultimate Test of a Pilot

It is easy to keep a good attitude when the weather is good. A test or a pilot is to be able to maintain a good attitude even when the ride is not so smooth. Can you keep a good attitude when the weather gets rough? Those "pumps" along the road are really trying to mess with your head. But, if you can keep your head straight and believe what those instruments in the cockpit are telling you, you will come ahead.

For some this comes easier than others. But whether we are talking about aviation related bad weather or the kind we encounter in our lives, the question remains the same. In either case it takes some practice and a decision on our part to "trust the instruments" and follow the indications of God's Word. Just like we have directions we can read from the instruments in the cockpit we have directions we can read from the Bible. If we trust the directions and follow them, all will be well. Remember, it's only a *temporary upset* and eventually the rough ride will be over. Until then, keep the good attitude and follow directions.

What is an "upset" anyway? It is a "set-up" upside down! That's exactly what the enemy does. He likes to turn everything upside down to **set** us **up** trying to get us **upset**. Don't listen to his devices. Just follow the true directions of the Word of God.

You have probably heard the acronym F.O.C.U.S., meaning Follow One Course Until Successful. That is exactly what you are to do when the rough weather surrounds you. Do not deviate from the good practices you know you should be following, which is trusting the instruments in order to keep the good attitude.

All of this holding a good attitude takes practice in aviation as well as in life. A good pilot wasn't just born a good pilot. There has been a lot of shaping along the way of learning good habits, good judgment (decision making) and skills. On the other side of the coin, the pilot could have adopted some less preferred habits, poor judgment and not have his skills quite up there yet and fall into the trap of following his senses.

Following your senses can get you into a heap of trouble as they can really mislead you to dangerous attitudes. This would be exactly what the enemy desires to do with us. He knows that if he can just mess with our heads and lead us to follow our feelings causing us to make poor decisions (judgment calls) he can lead us astray.

It can be very confusing if, instead of believing your instruments, you trust your senses, since they are telling you two different things. In aviation this could be fatal as the airplane could gradually develop a flight path of spiraling down to the ground and no-one would actually be controlling it. All the while pilot would be "feeling" that everything is under control.

It is also vital for us in our lives to develop a trust for God and His Word. If we don't, there may be two totally opposite signals coming from our senses (feelings and head knowledge) and the Word of God. That could get confusing as we *know* that the Word of God is the truth, yet at times the directions from the Word and from God does not make "sense". Just know this: it's not supposed to make sense, but it's supposed to make Faith, and it does. Now put it to work for you!

CHAPTER THREE

Wisdom Nugget #3

The Sun Will Shine
On Anybody Who
Will Get Out In It!

—Gloria Copeland

CHAPTER THREE

Mountain Be Thou Removed

If you are experiencing rough weather, just know that we have been given authority to tread on serpents and scorpions and over all the powers of the enemy. We have received of the Lord the instructions for life in His Word. If you simply trust Him and His Word and do what it says, you will get to the other side, to the destination that God designed for you. You have been given the authority to "steer your ship" and make decisions for your particular circumstances that you may be encountering in your life.

Since I fly, God often speaks to me from the point of view of a pilot. He always relates to people in terms of what they know and do in their lives. The following Word is one of those that came to me recently regarding our commitment to destroy debt in our lives.

My husband and I committed ourselves to seeding our way out to debt freedom so we will owe no man but love only. We have been seeking Him, studying His Word and spending time with Him as He is our Source for everything.

Every once in a while the things of life try to get your attention and cause you to look at things in the natural. You can't do this and expect miraculous results in whatever it is you are believing God for. Instead, you must stay steady on course and stay focused on His Word and His promises.

One morning while studying the Word I found myself thinking in the natural, mentally calculating how I could possibly pay off on schedule something I had committed to pay off in just few short weeks and also to eliminate all debt from our lives and own our home outright. The Lord graciously ministered to me the following Word and I want to share it here. It truly is from the point of view of a pilot and I certainly understood it seeing how small everything looks from above.

He said, "The mountain of debt is only a mountain to you if you look at it from below. Rise up and look at it from my point of view! It is but a small hill!

I have told you in my Word to HAVE FAITH IN GOD, *not on that mountain*. For verily, of a truth I say unto you, (put your name here), that WHOSOEVER (that's you), shall SAY to this "mountain" of debt (hill), Be thou removed and be thou cast into the sea and, and SHALL NOT DOUBT (in fear) in his heart, but shall BELIEVE that THOSE THINGS WHICH HE SAYS SHALL COME TO PASS, he SHALL HAVE WHATSOEVER HE SAYS.

Therefore, I say unto you (put your name here), WHAT THINGS SO EVER you desire (debt freedom, BLESSING, prosperity in every area…), WHEN YOU PRAY, BELIEVE that you RECEIVE and you SHALL HAVE. —Mark 11:22-24

Let this Word be **settled** and **established** in your hearts this day.

Wisdom is the **foundation**, **understanding establishes** it and **knowledge operates** it and makes my Word work in your lives. See Proverbs 3:19-20"

> ¹⁹The Lord by skillful *and* Godly <u>Wisdom</u>
> has <u>founded</u> the earth; by <u>understanding</u>
> He has <u>established</u> the heavens. [Col. 1:16.]
>
> ²⁰By His <u>knowledge</u> the deeps were
> broken up, and the skies distill the dew.
>
> —Proverbs 3:19-20 (AMP)

He also warned us how important it is in the light of His Word *not to speak ANYTHING in fear.* You see, fear is faith in reverse. Fear is faith in the opposite of that the good thing that God has promised. It is faith for God's promises not coming to pass in your life. YOU MUST RESIST THAT THOUGHT! Have faith in God instead!

> ²²And Jesus, replying, said to them,
> Have faith in God [constantly].
>
> ²³Truly I tell you, <u>whoever says</u> to this mountain,
> Be lifted up and thrown into the sea <u>and
> does not doubt</u> at all in his heart but
> <u>believes that what he says will take place,
> it will be done</u> for him.
>
> ²⁴For this reason I am telling you,
> whatever you ask for in prayer, believe

> (trust and be confident) that it is granted to you, and you will [get it].
>
> —Mark 11:22-24 (AMP)

The Word clearly says in Mark 11:23 that THOSE THINGS WHICH YOU SAY IN FAITH SHALL COME TO PASS. YOU SHALL HAVE WHATSOEVER YOU SAY *WHEN YOU BELIEVE* (saying in faith, not speaking in fear and having faith in the opposite of what God promised). CHOOSE FAITH and receive God's promises!

Whatever it is that you are believing God for, seek first His Kingdom and His way of doing things and all these other things will be added to you besides (Matthew 6:33). Trust in His Word and do not doubt. Then you **shall have** whatsoever you ask in prayer **believing** you have **received when you prayed**.

Have Faith in the System

Dr. Bill Winston has a great teaching called "Working the System" of the Kingdom of God. When you know how the system works, you have faith in it to do what you want or need it to do for you. The same way a pilot will study the systems of a particular airplane,

www.chickenwingscomics.com

so that he or she may have knowledge of the airplane's capabilities and have confidence in it to carry out what it was designed to do.

If you have not been learning about the airplane you are about to fly, you wouldn't have any idea as to how to operate it according to the Manufacturer's specifications. You wouldn't even know how to operate it normally. If you should now have an emergency, you'd be totally on your own trying to figure out what needs to be done to correct the situation. You can see how this could make things a whole lot worse and even detrimental.

The Manufacturer always provides an Operating Manual for the airplanes that they build. It is up to the operator to study the information provided so that the flight can be completed according to the Manufacturer's recommendations.

Chapter Three: Mountain Be Thou Removed

Just like the Bible has many chapters, in that Flight Manual you'll find different chapters. All of the information is necessary and required to operate the airplane safely. You could not leave anything out, or it would give you only partial information. Besides being illegal, it would also be unsafe to operate without all of the information necessary. The same way you cannot leave out anything from the Bible or you will have only partial operating knowledge and wisdom.

All of the information in the Bible came from the same Source, so also the information contained in the Flight Manual came from one Manufacturer. In that book you can find normal operating instructions, emergency operations instructions, systems descriptions, general information and limitations sections, performance capabilities of the airplane, weight and balance section, handling information for maintaining the airplane and so on.

You can see that all of the information is essential and is needed. For example, you wouldn't want the manual to exclude the *emergency section*, although you hope you never need to use that part of instruction. This information will cover any abnormal situations before they arise and it lets you know how to handle them should they come about. The *normal operating section* is simply a check list to be used in everyday operations and is therefore essential in itself.

The systems descriptions in particular are needed to understand how everything works. So, if something doesn't work as it is supposed to, you have at least a basic understanding of why a system is not operating normally and to be able to analyze the situation. The handling information for the airplane is needed, of course, for servicing it's many parts and to help maintain the airplane in an airworthy condition. General information and limitations sections give you more details of the particular airplane, of what it can and cannot do and further gives you the capabilities and the capacity of the aircraft.

Performance and the weight and balance sections in particular are to be consulted with, when determining if the airplane is able to perform in the current atmospheric conditions and still carry the load planned. Not totally understanding these two is one of the biggest reasons for accidents. You see, the plane is going to takeoff, fly, and land in "density altitude", which can greatly vary with different atmospheric conditions. I'll explain more about this important item next, but you can see already that all of the components of the book are needed for the safe operation of any flight. The same way, all of the Books of the Bible are needed to have the complete picture and revelation on how to operate the "System", the Kingdom of God.

What is this Density Altitude?

I'll give you an example. In Florida, where the temperature is usually much warmer than what is considered "standard" at sea-level, our density altitude is often 1000 to 3000 feet higher. This is where the airplane is *thinking* it is flying at. Other factors affecting our "density altitude" are humidity and barometric setting. The higher the humidity, the higher the density altitude is. The lower the barometric pressure is, the higher the density altitude is. So, when there is a low pressure in our region, the barometric pressure drops and the plane thinks it is flying at a higher altitude.

Why is this density altitude such a big deal? For one simple fact: when the density altitude is high, the air is thinner and the plane moves through the air a lot faster. This is important to know when you have a shorter runway for taking off or landing as you are going to require longer takeoff distance as well as landing distance. It is also nice to note that when the air is thinner, which it is at higher altitudes, your true airspeed is faster. This means that you are moving faster across the ground the higher you are since the atmospheric pressure around the airplane is getting lower the higher you fly.

The pressure around your airplane is always stronger at low altitudes and lessens with altitude. At the surface, the entire atmosphere is weighing on top of you. The higher you go, the less the air weighs, until in space you can encounter total weightlessness. So, think on your life with the Lord. The higher you get with Him, the lesser the pressure in life. But, if you hang around the low level devils, the harder it is and the pressure is on.

There is another side to this air pressure thing, and that is the performance of the airplane. At low altitudes the airplane's performance is improved, because there is a lot more air for the engines, which helps them produce more power. This same air also causes some friction on the airplanes surfaces and that translates to drag. When the plane climbs, the performance of the airplane actually reduces, but it will move through the air quite a bit faster and with more ease since the air is thinner at higher altitudes. So therefore, it doesn't need to put forth all that effort to move forward now.

I saw this as a direct parable in comparison to our lives with the Lord. When we are at a lower level, perhaps not having spent enough time with Him in His Word, we are really relying on our own efforts and our own reasoning rather than His. But, when we learn to trust in Him, let go and follow His leading and direction, that's when things start moving with more ease. No longer will we need to try and figure out our way of doing things. Instead, we will fully rely in His power to take over and much less of our own effort is needed. Yet we'll be moving along at a much faster rate, much like an airplane at a higher altitude where the surrounding pressure is less and the drag is reduced.

In conclusion, aim high and rest in the Lord. Life is much more enjoyable when you cast all your care on Him. Trust in Him and follow His lead. Read the Manufacturer's manual, the Bible, and operate according to the instructions written. Leave nothing out so you can have a complete revelation and knowledge of the System, the Kingdom of God, and how it operates.

CHAPTER FOUR

Wisdom Nugget #4

Debt Freedom Comes
Through Giving, Not Hoarding.
Selfless Acts Will Always
Pay Dividends.

CHAPTER FOUR

Weight & Balance & Aerodynamics

To make sure that the airplane flies as it is supposed to (or that it flies at all) you must do what we call weight and balance calculations. This is not only required by the regulations to be done before the flight, but it also ensures that the center of gravity, the balancing point of the aircraft, is where it makes the airplane aerodynamically able to be controlled by the pilot. There is a "safety zone" that we call weight and balance "envelope" where the center of gravity must remain.

If the balancing point is too far front or aft, there is a danger that the airplane could become *uncontrollable*.

The center of gravity too far in the front may make the airplane so nose heavy that upon landing the pilot may not be able to lift the nose high enough to land safely and may even hit the nose of the airplane to the ground upon landing. (I would call that a crash landing). On the other hand, if the center of gravity is too far aft, there may not be sufficient amount of control to recover from *any* unusual attitude as the control surfaces of the tail become less and less efficient and a crash may be the end result.

So you can see that the balance is essential when flying an airplane. Without balance it may be difficult or even impossible to recover from what we call a critical attitude that results in a stall. If there wasn't enough control from the tail section, the stall could very likely develop into a flat spin, which is impossible to recover from without the use of the tail section.

Critical Attitude

There is such a thing as critical attitude for any airplane. What the means is that at this attitude the airplane is unable to sustain a flight and is going to stall. The plane stalls really to release the excess load off the wings in order to avoid structural damage or weakening of the body and parts.

In flight we can increase this load by increasing the angle of attack of the airplane. We do this by raising the nose of the airplane up higher. If we raise it high enough, eventually the plane will reach its critical angle of attack, i.e. the critical attitude that will cause it to stall.

So why does the plane stall when it reaches this critical attitude? The reason is simple. If the load (or the weight that the wings are supporting) gets to be too much for the plane to carry, the airplane is designed to simply stall and release the load. It does this to protect itself.

When the plane stalls, not only has it reached that critical attitude that we call a critical angle of attack, but another thing takes place. There's what is called a *center of pressure*, also called *a center of lift*, which is carrying the airplane. When we increase the nose high attitude of the airplane, that center of lift moves gradually forward on top of the wing until it "runs out of the wing". During a stall it falls off the leading edge of the wings and it is unable to sustain the flight as we lose lift. If the plane didn't do that and stall it could end up with structural damage by exceeding the load it was designed to carry. Once the plane has stalled, though, it is designed to gain some more airspeed when the nose of the airplane falls downward. When it does that, it is able to raise the nose back up to normal attitude and fly out of it. However, this must be done gradually as to not over stress the airplane again.

This same thing happens to us if the weight of the world piles up on us to the extent that we cannot carry it any longer and we must release it. In essence, we stall for the moment in order to carry on and pick ourselves up again and fly out of it. Also, this relates to a critical attitude that we may have. Due to our own attitude we may cause unnecessary load and pressure in our lives. The manufacturer, God the Designer, has already built into us a "self preservation system" that causes us to get humbled in order to change our attitude when needed. This is only to protect us and is part of the design.

So, to avoid the humbling experiences, please operate the machinery according to the manufactures instructions and directions. This will save you from much trouble later.

Protect that Attitude

As a pilot, you get trained to recover from unusual attitudes. And as an instructor, you also get spin training. You must watch out that your students will not put you into unusual attitudes, including spins and you've got to protect that attitude.

So must you also see to it that your friends won't cause a wrong attitude in you. Don't let anyone upset you and cause in you an unusual attitude or a critical one! Else you won't be able to get too far ahead. Also, your passengers will be grateful and will stick with you when you keep a right attitude. If you don't, somehow or another, you may not have many friends along for a ride after a while.

Every pilot will try their best to keep the ride smooth for their passengers, but every once in a while outside circumstances may try to upset the attitude of the airplane. That's just life, but it doesn't mean that the crash must result. The pilot can still control the airplane's attitude and perhaps slow down a bit to keep it smoother to the passengers. As long as the pilot is following directions and interpreting the instruments as he has learned, he and the passengers will come out on the other side. So will you when you protect that attitude.

Failed Attitudes

You must also learn to recognize when your attitude is failing. In an airplane, it may creep up on us unawares and could be very detrimental if the pilot does not recognize this when it is happening. Originally, most airplanes had an attitude instrument, which was relying solely on what we call "vacuum" power, which is simply suction created by air. There is a vacuum pump, which is creating this suction, which in turn makes the gyroscope spin inside the airplane instrument. This gyro is supposed to always stay upright by spinning and therefore is used to compare the airplane's attitude to the horizon. This information is translated into the display, which is telling the pilot which side is up. You can imagine that if the pump fails and the spinning gyro slows down, gradually the display will tumble. This could happen so gradually, that if the pilot is not careful and does not recognize the failure of the attitude instrument, he will begin to follow the faulty indications and end up going in a different direction. If this continues for long, he may also end up losing the control of his airplane.

In the more modern aircraft we have quite a bit more attention getters installed to alert the pilot if something is failing or has failed. Almost immediately the pilot can be made aware of a failing instrument, especially in the electronic cockpits, where often an alert sound accompanies the visual cue about the fault. Once a pilot is aware of what instrument is not telling him the truth, he can either fix it, or if that is not an option, eliminate the problem by not looking at it for information.

You can also choose what you are paying attention to in life. Eliminate the sources that are leading you the wrong way. Stay focused only on what's right and true. Continual following of wrong signals is dangerous and could be detrimental to life. Learn to recognize what's right by studying God's Word, or the faulty information out there could get you unawares.

Performance

As important as weight and balance is the performance calculations of the aircraft. The manufacturer has determined what the airplane is capable of doing in any given set of circumstances. Particularly, this is important to the pilot when taking off or landing. The Manufacturer's Airplane Flight Manual has a Performance section in it, where a pilot can find out among other things how much runway is necessary for a safe takeoff and a safe landing.

These calculations are based on the takeoff weight of the airplane, outside air pressure temperature and the elevation of the field that the takeoff or landing is performed at. As you can imagine, if the pilot did not find out ahead of time this necessary information he could be taking off or landing and running out of runway midstream. Not a good thing.

Bible also tells us to plan ahead and count the cost before starting to build a house. Once you have done your preparations and know you are up for the task you can start your "takeoff roll". It is also important to count the cost before making a vow. Bible clearly says that it is better to have not made the promise than to regret afterwards and make excuses. In aviation this kind of thing could result in an accident, crash and the end of life.

Always count the cost and when you make a vow be prepared to pay it.

CHAPTER FIVE

Wisdom Nugget #5

Faith And Doubt Both Have A Frequency.
God Cannot Hear The Doubt Frequency.
He Is Not Tuned Into It.

CHAPTER FIVE

Law vs. Principle

As in the natural, so in the spirit there are laws we must follow. We all know about the Law of Gravity. We know that even if you didn't believe in it, you would fall down if you jumped off a building, because the Law of Gravity is always at work. Your belief then doesn't make the Law of Gravity ineffective. However, there are Principles in Aerodynamics that can overcome the Law of Gravity and that is called the Law of Lift. You must know something about the Aerodynamics to counter act this Law of Gravity and therefore overcome it.

Airplanes fly because of the Principles of Aerodynamics. It is not that the heavy piece of metal all of the sudden became of no weight, but the Law of Lift overcame the Law of Gravity and the Law of Lift operates based on the principles of Aerodynamics. The same way there are laws set in motion in the spiritual world, much like in the natural. We call them sowing and reaping, seed time and harvest. Once you recognize this you can change your harvest.

The Lord told me once that we so often limit ourselves with our thinking of what we believe we do or don't deserve, receiving only what we believe we deserve. If we only recognized that all we have and all we'll ever become is by the Grace of God and not by our own works. But often we are held back by our belief of not deserving something. All this really boils down to is believing that we receive only based on our own works. While there are consequences for all that we do and say, it is still by Grace and not by our works that we are saved or receive ANYTHING of the Lord.

So then, it is not the Law of Bondage that we have, but it is the Law of Result, Harvest and Consequence. Everything in the natural just like in the spiritual operates by this law. We call it the Laws of Sowing and

Reaping. Your faith is a seed, you sow in faith, in fear, or in belief and will reap accordingly. Your words are seeds that produce after their own kind (words of Faith, words of Fear, words of Doubt, words of Evil or words of Grace and Favor)

If we learn to operate by the Principles of Faith, we can overcome the Laws of Fear, Doubt and Unbelief and come out Victorious in the Word.

Put the Right Law in Motion

Although we are no-longer under a Law but under Grace, everything in this world is set in motion, everything follows a law. God didn't put away the law that He put in motion, but as we mentioned before it is not a Law of Bondage, but a Law of Result, Harvest and Consequence that we operate in.

In the natural and in the spirit there's a Law of Gravity and a Law of Lift and there's a Law of Sowing and Reaping. You put these Laws to work and the results will follow. Everything has a result for a harvest or a consequence.

Isaac Newton discovered this in science. His Third

Law is the Law of Reaction. It states that "**For every action, there is an equal** (in size) and **opposite** (in direction) **reaction** force". You could also state it by saying that for every motion there is an equal and opposite reaction. The action of the jet engine's thrust or the pull of the propeller pushes the air rearward and leads to the reaction of the aircraft's forward motion. The same way in the water, when you swim you push the water with your hands and your feet behind you and your body moves forward.

So for every action or force there is an equal and opposite reaction. If there is Gravity, there is Lift and if there is Fear, there is Faith. You choose which side of the Law you put to work for you. All you have to know is the principles behind them to make them work in your life. We can learn the principles from the Word of God and know beyond the shadow of a doubt how to operate in the BLESSING and harvest the good that God has promised to you in His Word. Since we mentioned Newton's Third Law, let's also look at the other two of his laws and how they relate.

Newton's First Law of Motion is the Law of Inertia. This law states that "A body **at rest** tends to **stay at rest** and a body **in motion** tends to **stay in motion** with **the same speed** and in **the same direction** unless acted upon by an **outside force**". The force with which a body offers resistance to change is called the Force of Inertia.

The outside force here is talking about a force greater than that, which is keeping it steady right now. When the Lift is greater than the Gravity, the plane climbs. When the Gravity becomes greater, the plane changes direction and descends. As two forces are equal, they balance (or "cancel out") each other and there's no movement up or down (there is rest) and when the thrust equals the drag the speed and direction remains the same (there is no change). So, the Law of Gravity then would continue to pull on any object, unless countered by an equal or greater, opposite Force of Lift.

Two *outside* forces are always present on an aircraft in flight: gravity and drag. The pilot uses pitch (the attitude of the airplane) and thrust controls (the power) to *counter* or *change* these forces to maintain the desired flight path. If a pilot *reduces power* while in straight and-level flight, the aircraft will *slow down due to drag*. However, as the aircraft slows there is a reduction of lift due to the reduced airflow surrounding the wing, which causes the aircraft to begin a descent due to gravity.

Can you see how your attitude and the power of your words can control your flight path in this life just like a pilot controls the flight path of an airplane with the attitude and power? Do you also see why we continually must speak God's Word out loud in order to keep our attitudes correct and to keep the enemy from slowing us down? Therefore, we must stay in the Word to fill our tanks to the full so we have what to speak out of. The source of our power, the gas in our tanks, is the Word of God.

This same law works in our lives. Just like the natural things follow this law, the things in our lives also tend to stay the same (at "rest") unless they are countered by a force greater than that which is holding them in place or keeps them going in the same direction. Watch therefore the forces that are pulling on you and make sure that they are of God, lest you be pulled away from the Word and from His presence. Don't let the cares of this world become greater than the Word of God inside you. Don't let offense win over the Love walk. The decision is ours to choose the direction that we take. Remember, the Lord has given us the free will and the authority to act as the Pilot in Command of our ship. He still is our Training Captain, but we must give him the respect and honor by letting Him be the final authority in our lives and trust and obey His command, His Word.

Newton's Second Law is the Law of Momentum. It says, "The **acceleration** of a body as produced by a net force is **directly proportional to the magnitude of the net force**, in the same direction as the net force, and **inversely proportional** to the **mass of the body**". What this is saying is that the stronger the net force affecting a body, the faster the acceleration is as it is affected by the force, and the heavier the body being moved is, the slower and harder its acceleration as it's resistance to the move is greater.

Acceleration here refers either to an *increase or decrease* in velocity, a momentum, although deceleration is commonly used to indicate a decrease. This law governs the aircraft's ability to change flight path and speed, which are controlled by attitude (both nose up or down and turning) as well as thrust (power) inputs. Speeding up, slowing down, entering climbs or descents, and turning are examples of accelerations that the pilot controls in everyday flight. So you also can control your direction and speed of your life towards your destination by controlling you attitude and the power of your words.

God's net force is greater than anything else in this

world, but don't you be a heavy resisting part of the body to Him by any means. Don't add weight of resistance through fear and doubt and by thinking and analyzing before you obey His directions. Be a light weight in that respect and be quick to obey. Have faith in His Word and His ability in you. This way He can accelerate you sooner in the direction that He wants you to go.

Talents

When God directed me to start writing this book, I chose not to be that heavy weight of resistance to Him. It was easier to simply accommodate Newton's First Law and remain in motion with the Lord. Besides this, I firmly believe that these inspirations to write have been direct answers to prayers that I have prayed asking God to show me how I could give more to God. It has been the cry of my heart ever since I fell in love with Him.

I particularly remember one instance when I was driving to work several years ago. I was on a fixed income and wanted to give so much more to God. I cried to Him asking, how could I ever give more when I was on a fixed income? I desired to be able to do so much more. Right then I heard God speak right into my spirit.

It wasn't an audible voice, but I heard it in my heart clearly. God said, "I did not give you the desires of your heart for you to just have them, but for ME to fulfill them". I was set free right then. I didn't know how and I didn't know when, but I knew that God had spoken and it was done. I knew I was going to be able to do ANYTHING that God Himself had placed in my heart.

Years later after meditating and pondering on His Word about the Talents in Matthew 25:14-30 and Deuteronomy 8:18 how He gives us the *power* to get wealth, I realized something. I put the two scriptures together and saw how God gave all of us talents according to our several ability (or willingness to use them and not hide them). Your talents can be traded into results like inventions, income and wealth. That wealth can be used to spread the Gospel and when you pay God's bills, He will pay yours! It's like a never ending circle. Whatever you give to God, He will multiply back to you, in finances, in ideas, in witty inventions, in favor, in any talents He chooses to give you. When you choose to use them for His glory, He will again bless it and multiply it back to you and so it grows as your ability (and willingness) grows.

I saw how our *talents* indeed were the *power* to *get*

wealth and if we use our talents wisely, He will trust us with more!

Years ago, when I was a new Christian the Lord had asked me which one of the servants was I going to be, when reading Matthew 25:14-30. I said, of course, I was going to be the one with the ten talents. At that time I took it literally thinking that we were talking about money and a business venture where you'd multiply by buying and selling merchandise. It could be that also, but it certainly is not limited to that alone. God is so limitless! There are ideas, inventions, songs and books and yes, even talented works of our hands that God has given us to multiply with. All this is to produce fruit for His glory. Remember, in ALL labor there is profit, it says in Proverbs 14:23.

So, God will give us power to get wealth. He gives us *talents* that translate into *power* to get wealth. Use those talents and don't sit on them! Be a wise and faithful steward of what God has given *you*. Then when you do something with what you have now, He can give you more talents to multiply with, because you are found to be a good and faithful servant.

Life is much like a game that's being played. If a team is to win the game, all of the players must participate and do their part. If God throws you a ball, catch it! Do what He tells you to do and as a team we all win the game.

All of us have been given talents according to our purpose. Use them, be faithful and diligent. Increase and multiply, be willing and obedient and you shall eat the good of the land. Stay in the game, do your part and don't drop the ball!

CHAPTER SIX

Wisdom Nugget #6

You Obey Him
When You Love Him,
You Love Him When
You Know Him.

CHAPTER SIX

What's Your Destination?

www.chickenwingscomics.com

In other words, what's your goal in life? Have you ever thought about it? Do you feel you are supposed to be doing something in particular?

We are all called to do something and each one of us has been given certain passions that are near and dear to our hearts. These passions should be our clue to what our calling may be and that just may be the way the Lord is leading you along your designed path.

No matter what your goals in life may be God is always leading us step by step. What I have found out, is that when you start following His leading, there's always something more in store for you. It will never get less in value, but it is always bigger and better plans for you, to bless you and those around you. But, the trip always begins with the first step.

In our last series we talked about flight planning, the preparation we need to do in order to reach the destination. We also talked about utilizing all the resources available to us to make the trip as safe as possible. We have continued to talk about some of those important subjects relating to the planning phase, such as calculating weight and balance and performance data in this book. In this chapter I wanted to bring out some of the items that could affect how high and how far you and your airplane can go.

First one, of course, is the **attitude**. You have most likely heard the saying "your attitude determines your altitude". This is for sure one of your most important aptitudes that will determine the quality of your travel through life and where you land. You see, just like an airplane, we also can have a variety of attitudes, and those attitudes will have an effect on the outcome of our efforts.

In aviation as we teach our students the basics of flying, we teach them to place the airplane into different attitudes using the flight controls and the power settings of the airplane. These are the tools we have, to place the airplane into an attitude that's needed for a particular result. For example, you want to take off and climb, the first thing you need to do is to position the airplane onto a runway and **point it into the right direction**. The second thing you need is to **add power** so that you can put it in motion moving forward and at the right airspeed, you need to move the nose of the airplane upwards into a climbing **attitude**.

So, you can already see that, right next to the attitude of the airplane, you'll need some **power** input in order to start moving forward and climb. We have already covered in the last series that attitude alone may not be enough to keep you afloat. You would also need the **power** helping the airplane to take off and to keep it climbing and moving along. So, the power then would be right next to the attitude that's needed.

This power may be within – like the engines that are part of the airplane – or it may be coming from the outside, like an updraft or lift, or it may be provided by another airplane that's towing a glider. Wherever it is coming from, it is needed to give us the necessary power to keep us flying and moving ahead. This power that we have in our lives is our words that we speak. They may be within us coming out of our mouths, or they may be words that we let others speak over us. Pay attention to those words and make sure they line up with God's Word!

The third thing that determines the power that an airplane has is the **number of engines** it has. Engines equal power, and the more of those you carry, the more power you can produce. So, if the power is in our words, are we going to have more power by having more words? No, not really. This is not what I was referring to with having additional engines. What I really mean by having more engines is that, having more Word of God within you is when you'll have a lot more power stored inside of you and that's like having more engines in your airplane.

So study the Word and get more of it in you. When that Word gets deposited into your heart, it will change the words that come out of your mouth. After all, it is in the power of those words coming out of your mouth and your attitude that determines your destiny and how fast you can get there.

Step by Step Plan

To get to your destination you should develop a step by step plan of action. This is called flight planning and in life and in business, it would be called goal setting.

In the Bible it is mentioned in Habakkuk 2:2-3 where it says the following:

> "And the LORD answered me, and said, <u>Write the vision, and make it plain upon tables, that he may run that readeth it.</u>
>
> For the vision is yet for an appointed time, but at the end it shall speak, and not lie: though it tarry, <u>wait for it; because it will surely come</u>, it will not tarry."
>
> Habakkuk 2:2-3 (KJV)

In other words, we are instructed to make plans, set goals and create goal posters to feed the vision that we may run with it and reach those goals. The people in the world are doing it, the high achievers are doing it! We know it works and it has been in the Bible all along.

If you follow these directions and write down your vision, which the Lord has given to you, then you will not be easily sidetracked when distractions come. Instead, you'll stay focused on the task at hand as you have set yourself a goal and a deadline.

We are using this same idea in flight planning. First we select our destination, and then we plan our route as to how we are going to get there. Then we calculate the time how long it will reasonably take us to reach our destination, determine the fuel necessary to get there and plan for any stops in between our departure and destination for refueling.

Sometimes we cannot reach our destination all in one flight, but must plan for intermediate stops for refueling. As you can imagine, these would be necessary steps for safety. Just the same way, you may have to plan on intermediate stops on your way to your final goal. We would call these our intermediate destinations or stops on our way to our final destination.

When you get to your intermediate stop, don't get comfortable and settle down if it is not your final destination. If you have large goals in your life, don't settle for anything less. And, if you think you have it made now, don't think you couldn't do any better! There's always room for improvement. If you stop now, it would be like exiting your airplane at your intermediate stop and never reaching your destination. This would be like stopping before reaching your full potential.

During our flight planning, we also prepare for anything unexpected with an alternate plan of action. The goal is still to get to our destination, and we have our plan of action to get there, but should there be some outside circumstances to interfere with our original plan, such as adverse weather, we plan for alternate plan of action for the benefit of safety and the best outcome. Remember, delays are not denials in life, neither is a diversion due to weather or mechanical break down a reason for not reaching our destination. So, it will not prevent us from accomplishing what we set out to do, but, it is simply a delay.

According to the Word, God has given all of us desires in our heart. In Psalms 37:4-5 the Word declares:

> "Delight thyself also in the LORD: and
> he shall give thee the desires of thine heart.

> Commit thy way unto the LORD; trust also in him; and he shall bring it to pass."
>
> —Psalms 37:4-5 (KJV)

In Amplified Bible the same verses read:

> "Delight yourself also in the Lord, and He will give you the desires and secret petitions of your heart.
>
> Commit your way to the Lord [roll and repose each care of your load on Him]; trust (lean on, rely on, and be confident) also in Him and He will bring it to pass."
>
> —Psalms 37:4-5 (AMP)

So then, it is God who gives us the desires of our hearts in the first place and then He Himself will bring them to pass if you trust and rely on Him and commit your way to Him.

I think of the Plan of God like this. First God plans the destination for each flight. The flights are the different missions that God has planned for each one of us. After that, God's Dispatch department will take over. The dispatcher's responsibility is to prepare the plan for each flight to reach the destination safely.

Chapter Six: What's Your Destination?

The dispatch would check the weather and make all necessary calculations for each flight (to prepare the way) and then dispatch the flights to send them on those missions.

Once the flights are ready to go, it's time to assign the crews to fly them. The Scheduling department would assign the crew members that are to fly the trips. This is when the calling takes place and a specific crew is chosen to take care of the mission. From the very beginning to the end, everything is team work. Without one, the mission would be incomplete. Just like in the body of Christ, we all have our job function and are fitly joined together to make it work as a team. No single person is called to do it all. All of us have different talents and strengths to backup each other. Therefore, we have been given different desires in life also as we are designed to attend to different tasks.

The desires you have are the clues to find out what God may have in store for us to do. God speaks to our hearts and not to our heads. You can hear Him with your inner Spirit. If you pay attention to that quiet small voice inside your heart and follow the step by step instructions, you will reach your destination and find out what God has planned for you. He only has good plans for us and has prepared that plan for us from the beginning. Now it is up to us to follow it.

Keep Your Eye on the Goal

The winners have a definite purpose in life and they focus on their planned future. They'll look *beyond* their current circumstances and they keep their eye on the goal, no matter what's going on around them. No distraction can defer them from accomplishing their determined purpose and goal.

This is exactly what a pilot does when he is landing an airplane. He must keep his eye on the end zone of the runway since that is the direction he is moving and that's the direction he wants to continue. If he takes his eyes off the end of the runway and focuses on what's right in front of him, he is most likely not able to judge the exact distance he is off the ground. Besides this, the ground seems to pass by a lot faster the closer you focus your vision. Therefore, it will be much harder to focus on anything and over controlling the airplane may be the result.

Because looking too close would make it much more difficult to judge how high you are above the ground, it will also be harder to know the precise time when to start leveling off the airplane's attitude above the surface. We call this "flaring", and we need to do this adjustment during landing in order to slow down the airplane's descend towards the runway surface. But, looking too close means you are looking down and not in the direction you want to keep going, it will be much easier to over control the airplane. If this happens, we are not going to finish smoothly. Most likely, we will not adjust our airplane's attitude in a timely fashion and a bad landing would result. It is possible that we could also bounce the airplane a few times up and down the runway before settling down, which would not be good for you, nor the airplane. Us pilots (and passengers also) want just one, smooth touchdown that makes landing look effortless, which it can be when you are one with your airplane.

Timing then is essential for flaring (leveling the airplane above the runway surface). If we level off too early and start adjusting airplane's nose higher and higher while being too high above the ground, we may stall the airplane. If this happens, the airplane will lower its nose in an attempt to recover from the stall. But, the problem is that while we are too high to flare, we are also too close to the ground for the airplane to have enough time to recover, and a crash will result if not corrected on time.

What we really aim to do is to get the airplane into what we call "ground effect". Ground effect is where the airflow around the wings and other control surfaces is changed in the way that it helps the airplane keep flying, even below those indicated airspeeds that it would normally stall at. Once in ground effect, we then "float" the airplane right above the surface until it slows down enough where it won't be able to fly any longer. When this happens, the airplane simply descends and settles down on the ground where we want it. As you can see, if you are not very close to the surface, it will be a hard landing. You just wouldn't want to slow the airplane down at 50 feet high and let it drop.

So, judging the distance from the ground is essential to landing. Therefore, a pilot must keep his eyes on the end zone and not try focusing on the fast moving surface below him. The same way, we are to keep our eyes on the goal of the high calling of Christ. If you stay focused on His Word, it will be hard for the devil to distract you off course and you'll be doing a lot smoother landings at your intermediate destinations also.

CHAPTER SEVEN

Wisdom Nugget # 7

The Instruction You
Obey Determines the
Future You Create.

—Nasir Siddiki

CHAPTER SEVEN

Stages of Development

There are parallels that relate to life, aviation and Christian development. As a baby when he or she grows into an adult learns initially to sit and stand, then walk and eventually run, the same way we develop our aviation students starting from baby steps into more advanced flight training. As a Christian also, we start off as a baby Christian, feeding on milk and hopefully eventually developing into a mature Christian, able to eat and digest meat of the Word and becoming strong in Christ.

Comparing this to an airplane, there are also similarities. As we discovered in chapter two, there are many types of airplanes, from small and less powered to more advanced and fast moving airplanes. If you are flying one of the smaller light airplanes, you are going to be limited as to how high you would be able to climb. If there is any weather around the areas you'll be flying in, you would definitely be affected. Most likely, you would not be seeing much out the window of your airplane during that flight and certainly not be in the sunshine. You would probably be stuck underneath the clouds and be surrounded with pretty grey outlook and not be able to see much different weather than others, who are staying on the ground.

But now, let's put you in a jet airplane that is able to climb on top of those clouds covering the sun and fly above the storms. Yes, during the climb out of those circumstances you will experience some rough weather, but that won't last for long. If you can endure that short season, eventually you'll be flying above the weather, and all the storms will be beneath you. After that, at least for the most part, the flight will be "smooth sailing". Above the storms the sun will be shining and the weather is nice.

Of course, we are not necessarily getting there overnight. Most students of aviation will not start off flying the jets and will be putting up with the limitations of flying the small aircraft, at least for a season. Besides, that's part of the training phase when we are usually flying the smaller airplanes anyway. However, those who have higher goals in mind and desire to fly bigger and more advanced airplanes will pursue their dreams and eventually get there.

Flying the advanced jets is not necessarily the interest of every pilot and there are enjoyable elements to flying the smaller craft also, like flying one in a beautiful weather at any altitude and enjoying the view.

Some pilots are so called "fair weather pilots" and will not be flying in adverse weather by choice. Of course, this is always safer anyway. At times it simply is a limitation of a particular pilot or an airplane as they are not certified or current to fly into any kind of weather. Whatever the case may be, this can apply to us also in our everyday christian lives, as all of us are a part of the body of Christ with different callings in life. While all of our parts in life are equally important, they may not seem to be equal tasks. Some of us may appear to be more advanced in knowledge and skill and may learn things easier while others seem to be struggling with those same tasks. None of this makes another of less value, but we are simply all created unique with different strengths and talents. Each one of us even has a unique finger print to prove that there is no-one else like us.

So, whatever your task and assignment is in life, don't take it lightly. Be diligent and pursue whatever the Lord has called you to be and do for this season. He that endures will receive the price for his obedience. The task is not the important factor, but obedience.

Situational Awareness

www.chickenwingscomics.com

As we are developing our flying skills and learning more about aviation, we are also developing something called situational awareness. At first, this is not usually something that comes very naturally as everything you see is new to you, and it is going to be a challenge to pay attention to everything all at once, when you are still trying to digest the new environment of aviation.

As a brand new pilot learning to fly, it takes all your focus and effort just to fly that airplane and you pretty much shut out all other things as a distraction to you. Meanwhile, there are other things that you should be paying attention to while you are controlling the aircraft since you are not the only one in the sky. This is why you'll have the instructor on board with you in the beginning, not only to teach you what you need to know, but also to bail you out of trouble that you could get yourself into by not paying attention.

Until you are ready to go at it alone without him coaching you along the way, the instructor will not let you go on a solo flight without him being right next to you. When you are ready to takeoff and land the airplane safely yourself, the instructor will endorse you to do that. He will step out and supervise you from the outside. While you are demonstrating your first solo flight, he will be watching you and listening to you on the frequency, making sure that you'll do and say things correctly. When you do, then more responsibility will be given to you.

What situational awareness is all about is, simply knowing at all times what is really going on around you and being aware of your surroundings. This includes listening to other pilots' transmissions on the radio announcing their locations and intentions, paying attention to ATC instructions and following them, knowing your own location in relation to other traffic and obstacles around you, especially when near any kind of terrain and airports, where there's most likely more of other traffic and so on.

Also, part of situational awareness is monitoring the airplane and paying attention to any signals telling you that something is not normal. As you gain experience, this will become easier and easier. Because you have *spent time* practicing, your flying skills are now becoming a second nature to you and you are beginning to *know* the airplane. The same way, when you *are practicing the presence* of God and *spending time* with Him, you are getting to *know* Him and get more in tune with Him.

You can immediately tell when something is not right and He can show you how you can correct whatever needs to be corrected. Just like you can fine tune your flying skills, you can fine tune your connection with God. All you need to do is spend time *practicing His Presence and spend time with Him!*

CHAPTER EIGHT

Wisdom Nugget #8

Following a Wrong Signal
Is Like Taking Offense and
Letting It Take You Down With It.

CHAPTER EIGHT

Respect and Honor

One morning as I was getting ready for work, the Lord began talking to me about respect and honor. For no apparent reason I was moved into tears just thinking about how grateful I was about my pastor and how honorable he is. I was thinking about all the things he has done in his life time, the sacrifices he has made serving our country and how he is now a General in the Army of the Lord helping us to learn the Word of God. He is always thinking about others. His heart is so beautiful and full of love. He is truly one of a kind. We are so blessed to have him as our pastor.

As I was thinking on these things, the Lord started

sharing with me how respect was your antenna for receiving. If you respect someone, you are ready and equipped to receive from that person. Without an antenna your receiver would be no good. Much like a radio or a receiver of any kind, without an antenna you couldn't receive whatever was being sent to you. So, if you want to receive from any man of God or anyone willing to teach you something, first there must be respect for you to be able to receive.

However, the antenna alone does not mean you will receive. It only means that you are ready and equipped to receive. You could respect someone for their beliefs, but not receive those beliefs to yourself by not accepting their message. There's something else then that must take place for your receiver to receive. The second thing, which the Lord shared you must have, is honor for that person. He said that honoring is like tuning your receiver into that person's message. In other words, you are accepting that message when you are tuning your receiver into it. Unless you tune into them and what they are saying, you cannot hear what they are saying. So, indirectly you are rejecting them and the message.

When you honor a person and the message, you are opening your spirit to receive from them. So, when a man of God, who is on a higher level, is sharing with you his revelation, you better tune in so you, too, can get to the higher level!

You may say how do you know whom you should listen to and what you should tune into? The same way like we do in aviation! We have resources like maps and information manuals giving you all the information you need, to navigate, operate the airplanes and tune into right frequencies along the way. All you need is to have someone teach you where to find all the needed information and how to use it. So also you must study the Information Manual, the Bible. Anything that will line up with the words of that Manual is worth listening to. Of course, you must understand the words you are reading, so you must have the Holy Spirit, the instructor, to help you study the Manual. All you need to do is ask. He is always ready and willing to help. Only respect and honor Him and you'll be able to receive from Him as your Teacher and Helper.

Tune into the Holy Spirit

If you are continually tuned into the Holy Spirit, you'll always be able to hear the message that is *of the*

Holy Spirit. In other words, you speak the same language. You'll be able to discern the messages that are of Him as they'll line up with the Word. The key is to be able to discern the right message, to identify it like a pilot identifies the right Morse code transmitted by the navigational aid, "Nav Aid" for short.

The pilots are provided with publications that we use to identify the Morse code that each Nav Aid transmits. A pilot wishing to navigate based on a particular Nav Aid Station must identify it first by comparing the signal it transmits with the information provided in the charts he must have with him. If you are not tuned into the right station, you'll receive a wrong Morse code. Therefore, if you fail to identify that the signal is incorrect, you'll end up following wrong directions and be led the wrong way.

Just like a pilot has been provided the materials to navigate the right way and the resources for him not to get lost, so have we been provided the tools necessary to follow the Airways of Life and they are based on the Word of God. Just don't allow the wrong message to lead you. Always be sure you're tuned into the right Station, which is the Holy Spirit, by identifying the message and comparing it to the Word of God.

Wrong Signals

Following a wrong signal is like taking offense and letting it take you down with it. It is easy to follow sense feelings, but fight the feelings that are destructive, such like offense, anger, disappointment etc. Accept only what's right information and keep flying above the circumstances of life. I know it's easier said than done, but the Word is telling us to stay away from being offended and therefore we have the ability and grace from God to do that. You must be able to overcome the wrong outputs that are trying to lead you down the wrong way and stop you from getting to your desired destination. Just like a pilot must fight the sensations of the wrong feelings produced by turbulent air around him, you must also, or the outcome could be disastrous.

Stay out of strife, because strife will keep you carnal. It will inhibit your ability to digest the meat of the Word. It is like listening to the sense feelings and overlooking what the instruments are telling you.

The entire purpose of the enemy is to shake your faith by sending you wrong signals. The devil's plan is to "shake your boat" so to speak, in order to have you let go of your faith. Don't listen to him! Trust in God's

Word instead. Only one side is telling the truth and it isn't the devil. There is no truth in him.

Have Confidence

It is promised to us in His Word, that if we simply have the *confidence* in His Word and ask *anything* according to His will He hears us and we'll have the petitions we desire of Him. So, if you simply study His Word and spend time with Him, you'll *know* what His will is and what has been promised to you. Then you'll have the confidence to ask what you will and have faith to receive it also, because you'll be asking according to His will. In John 15:7 Jesus said,

> ⁷If you live in Me [abide vitally united to Me] and My words remain in you and continue to live in your hearts, ask whatever you will, and it shall be done for you.
>
> —John 15:7 (AMP)

We also know it is His will for us to have His Holy Spirit to help us. It has been promised to us in John 15, so we can ask this according to His will. Particularly, in John 15:26 it is written,

> ²⁶But when the Comforter (Counselor, Helper, Advocate, Intercessor, Strengthener, Standby) comes, Whom I will send to you from the Father, the Spirit of Truth Who comes (proceeds) from the Father, He [Himself] will testify regarding Me.
>
> —John 15:26 (AMP)

So, if we know what His will for us is, then all we need to do is ask according to 1 John 5:14-15. This is what these verses say,

> ¹⁴And this is the confidence that we have in him, that, if we ask any thing according to his will, he heareth us:
>
> ¹⁵And if we know that he hear us, whatsoever we ask, we know that we have the petitions that we desired of him.
>
> —1 John 5:14-15 (KJV)

I especially like how Amplified Bible puts it:

> ¹⁴And this is the confidence (the assurance, the privilege of boldness) which we have in Him: [we are sure] that if we ask anything (make any request) according to His will

> (in agreement with His own plan), He listens to and hears us.
>
> ¹⁵And if (since) we [positively] know that He listens to us in whatever we ask, we also know [with settled and absolute knowledge] that we have [granted us as our <u>present possessions</u>] the requests made of Him.
>
> —1 John 5:14-15 (AMP)

So if you honor and respect the Word, you shall ask *any thing* according to His Will, including receiving the help from the Comforter, our Teacher, the Holy Spirit, which has been promised to us, then you *have* the petitions you ask of Him. Notice the present tense. You have it now, the moment you asked with confidence!

If you don't yet have what you are believing God for in some area of your life, you must not go by sight. You absolutely must have respect to the Word. Then you must honor the Word by not doubting it. Remember, we walk by faith and not by sight, just like a pilot who flies in the clouds. He is not able to see outside of his own surroundings inside the cockpit, but he has his instruments that he believes in and relies on. He cannot go by his sense knowledge or he is bound to lose control of that aircraft. He must stay focused on his instruments, just like you must stay focused on the Word of God.

If two indications do not agree, one of them is lying. In flight, if a pilot flies through a turbulent air and feels disoriented, it is either the feelings the pilot senses or the instruments that are telling the truth. All pilots know that it is not the feelings we must rely on, as difficult as it may be to ignore them. Following those feelings could get you killed. So, we trust and follow the cockpit instruments instead, especially when all of the instruments are telling the same thing, confirming each other.

In our case, it is either us or the Word of God that's telling the truth and it certainly isn't the Word of God that is lying. In the mouth of two or three witnesses let the Word be established, so also the pilots must confirm the instruments are telling the same thing when compared to each other. This way we can identify possible wrong signals and not follow them.

Revelation is what will give you the manifestation, so stay in the Word. Have confidence in it and get the revelation of it. This will give you possession of what you believe God for as you find your answers in His Word. God has so much more in store for you than what you could have ever dreamed or imagined possible.

CHAPTER NINE

Wisdom Nugget #9

We Are Today
The Total Sum of
What We Spent Time
Doing Yesterday.

CHAPTER NINE

Get Ready To Be Intercepted

On the wall of our church's sanctuary there is a digital display unit that is used during the service to indicate when there are additional volunteers needed in the Children's Ministry, or a particular number assigned to a child is shown, so that the parents know their presence is requested in reference to that child. Every once in a while numbers 7777 show up on the wall. This is the same exact number we use as a code when an airplane is being intercepted by military for wondering into a prohibited airspace. It's the number we call a "squawk code" that the military aircraft will display on their transponder units, so that the ATC can identify them on their radar that these are the intercepting military aircraft.

When the military aircraft intercept a wondering or lost aircraft, their job is to get that wondering aircraft's attention and lead it to a landing. You must submit to the authority of those military aircraft trying to lead you away from the airspace you should not have entered into in the first place. If you do not, it is going to be you who are in trouble with the law. There could already be consequences for wondering into an area you we not supposed to enter, no matter how ignorant you may have been about it. Usually the trespassing is innocent and unintentional, but the military will be finding out how the pilot ended up flying there and the correction will be made.

Every time I see this displayed on the wall, I think of God, Holy Spirit and His Holy angels intercepting us in the Church service and leading us into the right direction. If there was anyone going in a wrong direction, they shall be corrected and re-directed to follow the leading of God and the Holy Spirit.

Just like military is helping an aircraft that is lost and wonders into an unauthorized area by intercepting it and leading it for landing, God is also helping us by intercepting us with his Holy Spirit and His angels when we are lost and wonder into an area where we do not belong. He will lead us by His Holy Spirit away from danger and into His perfect will.

Now, that lost aircraft could be disobedient and decide not follow the directions of the intercepting aircraft. If they disobeyed and did not comply with the instructions, there would be serious consequences. The worst of it is, if you became a real threat, you could be shut down. So ignorance could be a real killer, couldn't it? Bible says this also when it states in Hosea 4:6 that

> [6]My people are destroyed for lack of knowledge:
> because thou hast rejected knowledge, I will
> also reject thee, that thou shalt be no priest to me:
> seeing thou hast forgotten the law of thy God,
> I will also forget thy children.
>
> —Hosea 4:6 (KJV)

We have all been lost at least once in our lives. What I mean by being lost is that until we asked Jesus to come into our hearts, we were lost in this world. But thank God for the intercepting aircraft which He sent to direct us into the right path! I am thankful that, as for me and my household, we followed God's military aircraft in to His Military Base. Because of that obedience, our background has now been cleared and we have been invited to be good soldiers in the Army of the Lord.

If you haven't yet done so, I am inviting you to do the same and follow the aircraft He sent for you. God is a good and merciful God and an awesome leader of His Army. He forgives mistakes and cleans up your past. Join us at His Base and leave the enemy's camp. The benefits and the rewards are out of this world.

Harvest

Now, notice that there is a harvest we reap from everything we do in life. We'll reap the results of our own actions and get the harvest from the decisions we make. Hopefully we'll know to make right decisions that lead to right actions.

But, if you know to do right and don't, there are consequences. Also, if you *do not recognize* what's right and do wrong because of it, there are still consequences. It's like going to sow some seeds that you *thought* would grow you a harvest of watermelons. But, what you thought was watermelon seeds were bad apple seeds. Instead of reaping a harvest of juicy watermelons, you'll have some rotten apples. Would it make any difference that you were ignorant to the fact that those seeds were not what you thought they were? Of course it wouldn't. You are simply going to reap what you sow, knowingly or unknowingly.

The key is then *learning* to recognize the seeds we sow, *knowing how* to make the right decisions and *choosing* the right ways because we love and honor Him, and *understand* the rewards and consequences of our actions also. How else would we do that except we spend time with Him and study the instructions given to us?

When a person desires to get a pilot's certificate, he is expected to study. If that person is lazy and does not spend any time studying, there is very little hope for him or her to ever accomplish the process of becoming a pilot. But, when you have someone who is eager to learn and ambitious to get his training accomplished in order to eventually be ready for his final test, you'll see that person continually studying and spending time in aviation. That person will take his training seriously and is continuously thinking about it. He is eating, sleeping and drinking aviation and therefore he is getting it into himself. In a way he is becoming one with it.

This is the same way a professional athlete will treat his profession. He "professes" to it all the time and practices, it is his life and therefore he is called a professional in his field. Although it may have started as a sport to him, it became a profession as he kept professing it. As Christians, we are also supposed to profess the Word of God and become one with it, because it is our life.

Have you ever noticed that with whom and with what you spend the most of your time with you'll become like? Even married couples eventually start resembling each other and shaping one another, whether they intend to or not. What you give the most of your attention to will *become* you. Your attitude and your thinking work the same way. We are today what we spent time doing yesterday. So, if you like what you see, keep doing what you've done all along. If you'd like to get a different output, make sure you'll change the input.

Pay attention to the people you admire and find out how they got there. There is a good chance that they did something and followed a pattern to reach that point. They are now reaping their harvest and we can always learn from them. This is especially true when God is using someone as an example to give us hope and teach us something. One thing is certain, that God is not looking for the most qualified person for His missions. He is simply looking for the one who is available and willing to do the task, someone who is eager to learn from Him and spend time with Him.

Life is all about sowing and reaping. The same harvest principle works in our lives the way it works for a farmer, so we'd better know how to sow good seeds so we can reap a good harvest. The best way to find out is to stay in the Word to "be in the know".

Air Force One

When an airplane carries the president of United States, the call sign for that airplane becomes Air Force One. Without the president occupying that airplane, it is just another airplane, although it is very specifically equipped, worthy to carry the president and adorned with many important details because of it.

If you are born again and have received Jesus Christ in your heart, then you are carrying the King of kings and the Lord of Lords. In a way *you are Air Force One* for the Lord! Even if you have not yet accepted Him as your Lord and Savior, you are well equipped and specially designed to become His dwelling place.

As the Lord gave me this revelation how in fact we are His Air Force One, I started to think about the fact how the Lord has literally blessed His people and the ministers of the Gospel these last days to fly their own airplanes so they can go where they need to go, when the Lord calls them to minister at a particular place at a specific time. Time is so short, He needed to do that. But, do you realize that when these ministers of the Gospel are flying these airplanes across the nation and the world, that there are literally bunch of Air Force Ones in the sky? Every airplane carrying a minister of the Gospel or a born again child of God is an Air Force One for the Lord.

Now, this revelation made me think of airplanes in a whole new perspective. Imagine, every time you board and airplane, it becomes a very special flight. That flight is literally carrying the King of kings and the Lord of lords. Your flight is protected by any means available. Besides that, you'll be surrounded by His security forces wherever you go. It's better than the real thing! Remember, the Word says,

> [16]Behold, I have created the smith who blows on the fire of coals and who produces a weapon for its purpose; and I have created the devastator to destroy.
>
> [17]But no weapon that is formed against you shall prosper, and every tongue that shall rise against you in judgment you shall show to be in the wrong. This [peace, righteousness, security, triumph over opposition] is the heritage of the servants of the Lord [those in whom the ideal Servant of the Lord is reproduced]; this is the righteousness or the vindication which they obtain from Me [this is that which I impart to them as their justification], says the Lord.
>
> —Isaiah 54:16-17 (AMP)

CHAPTER TEN

Wisdom Nugget #10

Amateurs Will Practice
Until They Get It Right,
The Professionals Will Practice Until
They Don't Get It Wrong.

Unknown

CHAPTER TEN

In Conclusion

Let's recap here what we have learned so far. First of all, if you want to learn to fly, you must have a teacher to teach you. To receive from him, you must have a trust relationship and you must be able to respect and honor him. For us to fly through the airways of life, God has provided us such a Teacher, His Holy Spirit, to train us in the knowledge of Him. We can totally trust and rely on Him and we know that He will never fail us, nor forsake us.

He has also given us many natural teachers. We call them pastors and teachers, the ministers of the Word of God. If you respect and honor whom God has sent, you will be able to also receive from them.

Secondly, you can be a pilot at different levels. No-one gets started from the top, but everyone begins with the first, initial certification and as the skills begin to improve and dedication continues to grow, you are able to graduate to the next level. You can go as far as you want to go with courage, commitment and consistency. Just dedicate yourself to be faithful to the desire that God has put in your heart to achieve. He will do the work through you.

You can also be a glider, a prop plane, or a jet. All will fly, but how far you want to go determines who you need to be.

When you fly and have placed your airplane in the right attitude, don't forget to trim the airplane. This will keep the pressures off that may try to interfere with your attitude and prevents additional attitude adjustments.

Remember, it is easy to keep a good attitude when the weather is good. But, occasionally even the best pilots will encounter "pumps" along the road that are really trying to mess with your head. If you trust your instruments and keep a cool head, you'll be fine. "Upset" is really a "set-up" spelled upside down. It's a setup! Don't fall for it.

Even airplanes fly with much more ease at higher altitudes since the air is thinner and the friction is less. Therefore you, too, must aim high and rest in the Lord. That's where there's a lot less resistance.

Read the Manufacturer's manual, the Bible, and operate according to the instructions written. Leave nothing out so you can have a complete revelation and knowledge of the System, the Kingdom of God, and how it operates.

Being balanced is essential to flying an airplane and piloting in the airways of life. Avoid a critical attitude, as this could lead to a stall. It could be a humbling experience. Protect that attitude at all times and watch out for failed attitudes.

Count the cost before you start your takeoff roll. Make sure you are prepared for the task before you make a vow. It is better to not make a vow than to make one and not be able to keep it.

When you know God's aerodynamics, you know you can overcome the devil's Law of Gravity with God's Law of Lift. Simply put the right law in motion. Everything has a result for a harvest or a consequence. So for every action or force there is an equal and opposite reaction. If there is Gravity, there is Lift and if there is Fear, there is Faith. You choose which side of the Law you put to work for you.

God will give us all talents. Those *talents* will translate into *power* to get wealth. Whatever your talents, use them wisely, and whatever you do, don't sit on them. Stay in the game and don't drop the ball!

There are three things that determine how high and how far you can go. The first one, of course, is the attitude, the second the power, and the third, the number of engines. Your attitude determines the altitude, and so does the power of your words. The Word of God is like having more engines and the more Word of God you have in you, the more power you have in those engines.

Keep your eye on the goal. The winners have a definite purpose in life. They focus on their planned future and look *beyond* their current circumstances.

As God is developing us from a baby christian to a mature one, on the way there, you may need to endure a rough ride. It is really because we must develop our resistance to the outside circumstances and while learning to walk, we are developing that balance we will need to walk upright. But, just like a pilot, who in the beginning had to endure the rough weather at lower altitudes, now just needs to ride through it few minutes on his way to the top. Afterwards he will enjoy the sunshine and calm on top of the storms.

Watch out to never take offence. It would be like following a wrong signal and letting it take you down with it. Instead, respect and honor the messenger and the message. Otherwise, your receiver cannot receive His message since without honoring it, you cannot tune into it.

When you receive it, receive it with confidence. If you honor and respect the Word, you shall ask *any thing* according to His Will, He hears you and you shall have the petitions you have requested from Him.

Life is all about sowing and reaping. Make sure you *know* the seeds you are sowing. We will all reap our own harvest from the seeds we have sown, whether we recognized what we sowed or not. Every seed at the end produces after its own kind.

Lastly, if you are lost, get ready to be intercepted. God is faithful and just and He has your best in mind. Trust in Him and follow Him. The benefits and the rewards are truly out of this world. And yes, you too, can become Air Force One for the Lord.

My Prayer

My Prayer is that May God Richly Bless You and Yours as you have given to His Work through this book and May the Lord lead you in Your Designed Path of Life for His Glory.

About the Author

Tarja Newman is a licensed Airline Transport Pilot with Advanced Ground Instructor license and Gold Seal Flight Instructor ratings entitling her to teach Single-engine, Multi-engine and Instrument Pilot Curriculums. Currently she is serving as an Assistant Chief Pilot at a local Flight School in South Florida. She has also worked as a crewmember in the airline industry and owned several businesses, but somehow her passion of teaching has always led her back into training others, both in aviation and in business.

Her passion in life is to find wisdom and pass it on to others as it relates to everyday life both personally and professionally. She credits all wisdom to the Word of God, which is the basis of her life and by which all things were created.

In the beginning was the Word…
and the Word was God…
All things were made through Him…

— John 1:1-3

Then God said… and it was so.

— Genesis 1

Prayer of Salvation

If you are not absolutely sure and *know* that you are going to Heaven, pray this following prayer with me.

Heavenly Father, I come to you in the Name of Jesus. I believe that Jesus died on the cross and rose again from the dead, so that I might have ever lasting life. Therefore, I ask you to forgive me of all my sins that I have ever committed. Jesus, come into my heart. Fill me with the power of Your Holy Spirit and lead me in the way that you designed me to walk in. I believe I am saved.

In Jesus' Name I pray, Amen.

To contact us at Blessings Storehouse Ministries you can write to us at blessingsstorehouse@gmail.com or visit us at http://blessingsstorehouse.blogspot.com.

If you are a minister of the Gospel of Jesus Christ and would like to use the books for fundraising purposes, you can contact us directly for more information.

www.ingramcontent.com/pod-product-compliance
Lightning Source LLC
Chambersburg PA
CBHW061442040426
42450CB00007B/1177